BAKELITE JEWELLERY

BAKELITE JEWELLERY

A Quantum Book

Published by Grange Books
an imprint of Grange Books Plc
The Grange
Kingsnorth Industrial Estate
Hoo, nr Rochester
Kent ME3 9ND

ISBN 1-84013-274-4

This book is produced by
Quantum Books Ltd
6 Blundell Street
London N7 9BH

Project Manager: Rebecca Kingsley
Art Director: Siân Keogh
Project Editor: Jo Wells
Designer: Martin Laurie
Editor: Lyn Coutts

The material in this publication previously appeared in *Bakelite Jewelry*

QUMCCBJ
Set in Gill Sans
Reproduced in Singapore by Eray Scan Pte Ltd
Printed in Singapore by Star Standard Industries (Pte) Ltd

CONTENTS

INTRODUCTION

BAKELITE – A COLOURFUL HISTORY

BACKGROUND Celluloid cherry necklace and bracelet.

All components of this leaf set were moulded from celluloid. A close look reveals the mould marks.

Jewellery-making, perhaps one of the oldest crafts, began when people began to adorn themselves with natural objects, such as stones, feathers, nuts shells and leaves. Prehistoric peoples gathered beautiful and colourful or symbolic items and linked them together in some crude way. Adornments may have been intended for symbolic or religious purposes, such as the headdresses of healers or priests, or the wearing of certain items to denote mourning or marriage. Jewellery has also been traditionally used to show wealth and as a gift in many cultures.

The jewellery-maker eventually became a craftsperson, moulding and changing natural objects and using his own imagination to weave his own personality and style into the pieces. Like the other crafts the skills would have probably been passed on to an apprentice. After working well with the master for a while, the apprentice eventually would have devised a style and would eventually fulfil commissions of his own. The imaginations of early artisans and their successors would grow in leaps and bounds. Soon, the rocks became gemstones, the fastenings or findings became brass, copper, gold, or silver. The jewellery-maker found that the earth is a wonderful supply house.

The reliance on natural materials persisted until the mid-nineteenth century when chemists and scientists began to discover substances that could be substituted for expensive or rare bounty from the earth such as amber, ivory or gemstones. Gutta percha (a natural material), celluloid and galalith are the bridge between natural and man-made materials, with Bakelite being the first entirely man-made product without equal in the natural world.

Gutta percha

By the nineteenth century gutta percha, a combination of proteins from the Malaysian rubber tree with various fillers, was being used for hundreds of purposes, one of which was jewellery-making. This material, which is extremely hard but rubbery, was moulded or carved to create the design. Since gutta percha is mostly black in colour it was used extensively for mourning jewellery; black, brown, and a rare greyish-brown gutta percha was used for picture frames and household accessories.

Because gutta percha dries over years of exposure, it is rare to find any pieces that have not been repaired. If you happen across a perfect example, check it carefully – it is likely to be simply a case of mistaken identity. Gutta percha is often confused with celluloid, bog oak and even amber.

Celluloid

While the nineteenth century progressed, so too did the developments of semi-synthetic plastics. In 1842, a Swiss chemist by the name of Schoenbine developed cellulose nitrate – a mixture of sulphuric and nitric acids. to which was added sawdust and cotton fibres to produce an explosive substance. But Schoenbine's invention was to have a more wide-ranging impact.

In 1853 Englishman, Alexander Parkes experimented by introducing camphor into cellulose nitrate and produced a flowing substance that could be moulded into different shapes. Once the thinners dissipated, a solid mass remained which retained the shape of the mould into which it had been poured. Parkes marketed his discovery under the name of Parkesine.

Misfortune plagued Parkes and he lost his patent rights to the American John Hyatt and his brother Isaiah. They called their invention celluloid and it was regarded as a miracle of science. Celluloid found many applications in household items, such as handles for silverware, picture frames, and dresser sets.The fashion industry took celluloid to its heart creating hair combs, hat ornaments, buckles, buttons, and jewellery, all resembling tortoiseshell, amber and even ivory. In fact the French developed a method of cross-hatching celluloid in quite convincing mimicry of ivory, known as 'French Ivory'.

The methods and techniques perfected by the Hyatt brothers are still in use today. Extrusion produced bracelets. Blow moulding produced hollow items and pins and earrings and necklaces were made in moulds.

ABOVE This patriotic army soldier, marketed as 'My body' pin is made from celluloid.

CENTRE AND BELOW Examples of fine celluloid lockets in pristine condition are very rare.

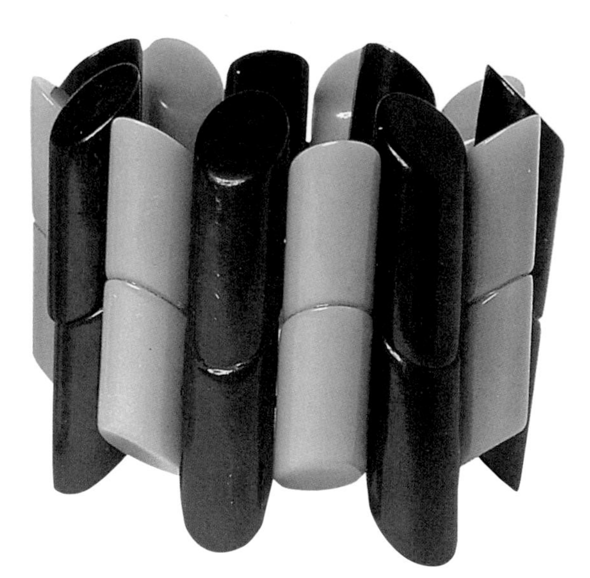

RIGHT Chunky cylindrical rods of dark and light make up this celluloid bracelet.

Galalith

During the 1890s, technicians were dabbling with different plant and animal proteins in the search for the new 'miracle plastic'. One such inventor was a German chemical engineer, Adolph Spitteler who was looking for a substitute for horn.

A blend of formaldehyde and cassein (a protein derived from spoiled milk) created an extremely hard material. He patented his discovery in 1897 and dubbed it galalith. Because galalith lent itself easily to carving and it would readily accept a high and lasting polish it quickly made its way into the fashion industry, being used as a base for buttons, dress clips, hat ornaments buckles and jewellery. Because of it hardness it also found application in commerce and industry.

Thermoplastics

Celluloid and galalith, are semi-synthetic thermoplastics. This means that when heated their chemistry changes and as a result they can be moulded into different shapes. By pouring the heated mixture in to carved moulds a great many different shapes could be turned out in large numbers. Different polymers were used for particular objects, depending on their pigmentation, hardness or durability.

Because the charge that bundles the fibres of thermoplastics together is weak and cannot withstand heat, a thermoplastic can be reheated and reformed, even though it has been cured. The molecules slide by one another under reheating, producing the flowing nature of hot plastics.

RIGHT An assortment of Bakelite and galalith novelty animals. Some have deteriorated quite badly.

DR. LEO HENDRICK BAEKELAND

Leo Baekeland was born in 1863 in Belgium, and attended the Technical School of Ghent. In 1880 he matriculated to the University of Ghent where he gained a Bachelor of Science degree and later a doctorate in natural science. He stayed at the University several more years, as a professor of chemistry and physics, also winning prizes and honours for his work.

Dr. Baekeland emigrated to the United States in 1889. As a means of support, he took employment with a photographic firm. While with this firm, he continued experimenting in his own laboratory at home, where he eventually formulated a light-sensitive photographic paper, which he patented under the name Velox. From 1893 to 1899, Baekeland headed his own firm, the Neperd Chemical Company that produced Velox and other papers and chemicals for the photographic trade. In 1899 he sold his company and the patent rights for Velox to the Eastman-Kodak Company.

Unemployed, but extremely well off, Baekeland continued his research and developed an electrolytic cell for the Hooker Electrochemical Company. By this time, Baekeland had set up residence in Yonkers, New York, where he had a laboratory, so he could further his research on shellacs.

The condensation of products emanating from the union of carbolic acid (phenol) and formaldehyde had been researched by Adolf von Baeyer in the 1870s. Von Baeyer had abandoned this work because the tedious process yielded an inferior product.

Dr. Baekeland used the thoughts behind von Baeyer's studies, but added various bases and a soluble solution to perfect the first phenolic resin and the first thermosetting plastic. Production started in his Yonkers garage in 1907 and operations were moved to Perth Amboy, New Jersey in 1909. By 1930 thousands of pounds of resin were being produced in an extensive plant at Bound Brook, New Jersey, as well as from plants in England and Germany.

LEFT Dr Leo Baekleland who probably never dreamed that his phenolic resin would prove to be such a popular material for the crafting of jewellery such as the beads shown in the background.

BACKGROUND Cast phenolic tubes with a bird motif running through the middle rather like a stick of rock, that when sliced were probably destined to become buckles and pins.

Thermosetting products

Until the discovery of phenol-formaldehyde, semi-synthetic plastics were all of a thermo nature. Products made from semi-synthetic plastics when exposed to heat would melt down again and distort, and could be 'recycled' for other purposes. What Baekeland discovered was a substance that, through extreme heat and pressure, could be cast or moulded into a product that could not be remelted. This is classified as a thermosetting plastic.

Bakelite was the first totally man-made element plastic. Because of its specific resistance to melting, it immediately became the main staple of the electronics industry. Bakelite will never melt or ignite, no matter how much heat or voltage is applied. It will, however, take on a burgundy-coloured mark if subjected to an open flame or extreme heat.

BELOW Bakelite handles on this child's knife and fork set, have mould-injected Scottie dog decoration. Once white, oxidation has caused the discolouration of the dogs.

The Bakelite accident

While working to create a particular plastic that could be substituted for shellac, Baekeland mixed together carbolic acid and formaldehyde. When he tried to reheat this formula, he discovered that it would not change form, no matter how high the temperature. The concoction was not only different to those produced by his fellow chemists, it was a totally new type of plastic. He patented his discovery, of the plastic that once set would never melt – Bakelite – in 1907.

Bakelite, its inventor soon discovered, could be cast or moulded. Casting, the method used to create most Bakelite jewellery, uses extreme heat and pressure to thrust forth a cylinder, tube, rod, or sheet with a cross section in the shape of, for example, a bird. The tube is then sliced into several bird-shaped disks.

A myriad of applications

Moulding is a process in which molten polymers are poured into carved moulds, creating shells for telephones, radio cabinets and containers. When the endless possibilities for the use of Bakelite instead of traditional materials, such as wood, stone, and other semi-synthetic plastics, became obvious it began to be promoted by Baekeland and his public relations people, as 'the material of a thousand uses.'

The world quickly embraced Baekeland's brain-child and the first of many companies to knock on

Baekeland's door were the electrical companies which had been looking for an insulator – a product which would not melt when exposed to heat and could be used to protect electrical parts. Plugs, electrical boxes, handles for electrical units and telephones were the first offspring of Baekeland's resin.

Most of the original Bakelite pieces were produced in brown, black and occasionally, clear amber. Baekeland experimented with wood flour, cotton fibre, asbestos and even metals to strengthen the emulsion. He quickly found that fillers could enhance the colour as well as strengthening the object.

The marketing department were soon able to start to offer Bakelite in an array of colours other than the standard black and brown. The Bakelite rainbow grew to include, red, green orange and white. Manufacturers of household goods could now cast things in living colour. Pot handles, spatulas, eggbeaters, bowls, dishes, cups, and saucers all took on the Bakelite colours of red, green, orange and white in plain or pearlescent finishes or swirly patterns.

An ubiquitous material

It was during the Roaring Twenties that American women were first tempted with Bakelite jewellery. Many was the flapper that dazzled the crowds in a speakeasy with multi-coloured Bakelite beads and bangles. Even the electronics industries relished these new colours. The drab browns and blacks were ousted by burgundy, red, and yellow radios, phonographs and televisions with amber knobs. As a promotion point Baekeland compiled a list of about 40 industries that could implement his resin, but within just a few years it was harder to formulate a list of 40 industries that did not use Bakelite.

Bakelite was ubiquitous in everyday 1930s life. From daybreak to nightfall, Bakelite was a finger or arm's reach away. It was used for more functional items that can be listed here – alarm clocks, toilet seats, toothbrush and shaver handles, hairdryers, kitchen utensils and dishes.

Just as important was the role Bakelite played in providing beauty or whimsical diversion from the economic gloom of that decade with brightly coloured, sometimes eccentrically designed items, such as radios moulded in the shape of Mickey Mouse and a host of beautiful and affordable costume jewellery. By the end of the 1930s, the challenge was to find a use that Bakelite could not be put to!

With the Bakelite revolution in full swing, not even the introduction into the market by the Catalin Corporation of a new pigmentation process dented Bakelite's success. If anything, it enhanced it and confirmed that the man-made materials were here to stay.

BACKGROUND Functional yet full of humour and whimsy are these Bakelite napkin rings. One even comes with a set of wheels!

BELOW Jade-coloured Bakelite key ring with the familiar Scottie dog decoration.

CHAPTER ONE

NECKLACES AND PENDANTS

Bakelite necklaces range from the simple and understated to the outlandish and bizarre. Pendants were probably the first neck pieces, with beading following close behind. Bakelite pendants were hung from either metal or celluloid. As in the other categories of jewellery, the metal signifies the European contribution, while the Americans found celluloid chain less expensive and easier to assemble.

Extant are many more beaded pieces than extensively carved or geometric designs. The beads – spherical or oval-shaped – were cut from cast cylinders and rounded according to the shape of the design. Whatever carving the designer had in mind was done at this point. There are examples of faceting (cutting faces into the beads as is done with gemstones), as well as floral carvings. When carved and ornament complete, the pieces were tumbled in huge drums containing fillers and various grit silica to a finely-polished finish.

Drilling was the last thing to be done. It was done in a machine that had a drill on each side. The two drills would work toward each other to create the hole.

ABOVE Plain, spherical beads strung on a metal chain, an example of Bakelite jewellery at its most understated.

LEFT Bakelite and celluloid in combination in this Victorian revival pendant. The cameo and chain are celluloid, while the black mount behind the cameo and the clear backing are Bakelite.

BELOW A subtly decorated neckplate piece hung on a metal chain.

BELOW Intricately-carved roses on what were once white Bakelite beads, interspersed with large, spherical black beads.

The size of the hole varied according to what material would be used eventually to link the beads together. Cotton was the most used fibre, but restringing was common as the cotton would wear and rot. Some of the European productions were strung on chain or were affixed to metal findings.

American neckwear seemed to be fashioned to keep away the blues. More boisterous than European designs, American jewellery designs had a sense of fun and frivolity almost verging on cheekiness. The popular fruit-and-vegetable style of Bakelite bracelets, for example, carried over into neckwear.

Though the European and American schools of design were often at variance, there are examples of crossovers. There are the stylish and deadly serious geometric necklaces that were produced in the States, and the tool necklaces that emanated from Germany.

BELOW A necklace consisting of elongated and lightly-faceted beads and spherical beads.

Both Europe and the States shared in the Victorian revival, and the Americans embraced the fluid and then the mechanical styles of the Art Deco era.

LEFT This beautiful necklace, bracelet and earrings set most probably came from Europe. The Bakelite egg-shaped beads have metal findings.

ABOVE Elongated disks cut in half are the main element in this multi-coloured geometric necklace.

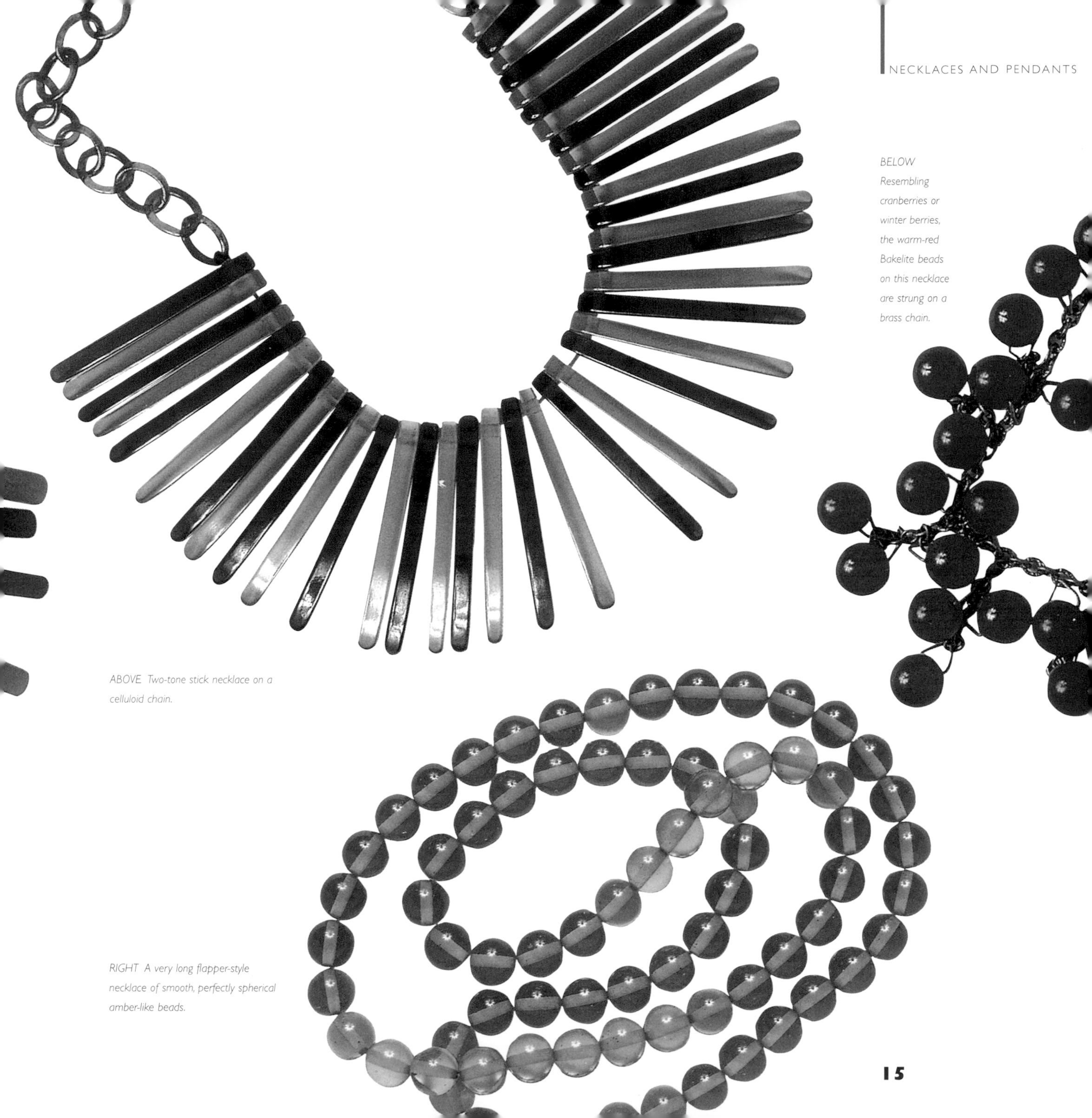

BELOW Resembling cranberries or winter berries, the warm-red Bakelite beads on this necklace are strung on a brass chain.

ABOVE Two-tone stick necklace on a celluloid chain.

RIGHT A very long flapper-style necklace of smooth, perfectly spherical amber-like beads.

RIGHT Faceted necklace of geometric elements are given a rustic look with marbled Bakelite.

BELOW The new man-made materials could be made to look like anything. This lovely necklace, on a celluloid chain, is faux tortoiseshell.

RIGHT Fruit-inspired designs for necklaces and even pins were very popular. The cherries and leaves are carved Bakelite, the chain is celluloid.

CHAPTER TWO

BRACELETS AND BANGLES

LEFT Heavily-carved bracelets with relief patterns of leaves and flowers.

BELOW Undercarving flowers with a rotary-type tool on the inside surface, gives this bracelet a 3-D look.

Bracelets are probably the most diversified member of the Bakelite family. Coming in all shapes, sizes, colours and designs, they are more plentiful and therefore easier to find than pins, earrings and all other pieces combined.

The bracelet was in all likelihood the first form of Bakelite jewellery produced. This is because of the ease in which it could be manufactured. The simple, plain and narrow bangle came on the scene during the 1920's and by the mid-Thirties was transformed into the wide, thick and 'carved to death' pieces that are so sought after today. (There's more about bangles on pages 28-30.) As time progressed, so did the design of Bakelite bracelets. Companies that had previously restricted their business to carving wood products, retooled and expanded into the Bakelite market. Their designs were simple to start with, but soon the better carvers were working on complex designs that would be reproduced in Bakelite form.

From tube to bracelet

After the bracelet or bangle was appropriated from the tube, it was put onto a jigging machine. The indexing head would calibrate the carving into windows or scenic sections. The carving was done with a range of tools – in a lathe and turned to the desired pattern, or a rotary-type tool was used in conjunction with a tracery mechanism to cut less complicated patterns.

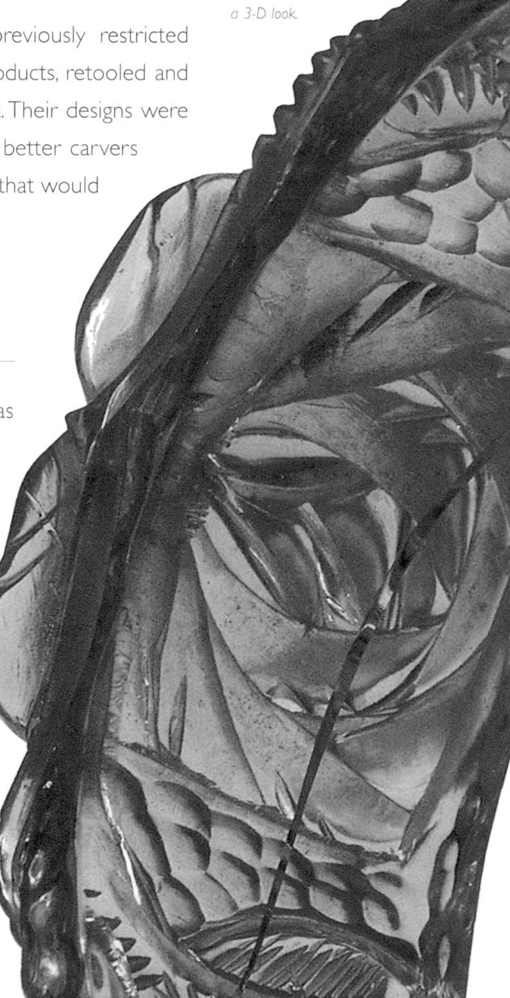

The more complicated, heavy relief pieces were pattern-scribed first, then were finished off with a rotary tool. This could be used to carve and get under the backs of, say, a rose, so that the petals stood in relief to get a 3-D effect. The rotary tool was also utilized freehand to carve most of the 'reverse-carved' pieces.

After the carving was finished the piece was tumbled in huge drums containing fillers and various grit silica. Each piece went through a rough, medium and fine process before a final detergent and polishing stage.

ABOVE A square bangle with an oval hole that could easily be a fashion item today.

Some pieces were polished with a cloth- or felt-wheel using a pumice solution to diminish any 'wheel' or carving marks before engaging in the cleaning and polishing stages. A few select pieces had the extreme edges finely polished to produce a glass-like finish; the carved sections having a beautiful matte-like or frosted finish.

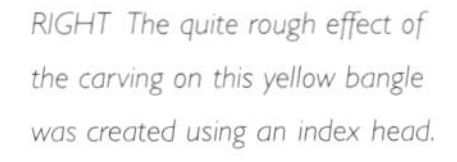

RIGHT The quite rough effect of the carving on this yellow bangle was created using an index head.

BELOW AND BELOW RIGHT Constrasting examples of a plain bangle and one with very simple scoring in the same vibrant red.

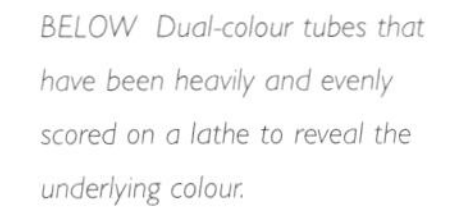

BELOW Dual-colour tubes that have been heavily and evenly scored on a lathe to reveal the underlying colour.

LEFT Smooth, rounded and polished exterior with an undercarving of flowers and foliage on the interior of this clear Bakelite bangle. The undercarving has been painted.

RIGHT Simple plain bangles were popular worn as spacers between ornate bracelets, or as a group that would make an attractive clanking sound when they jangled together.

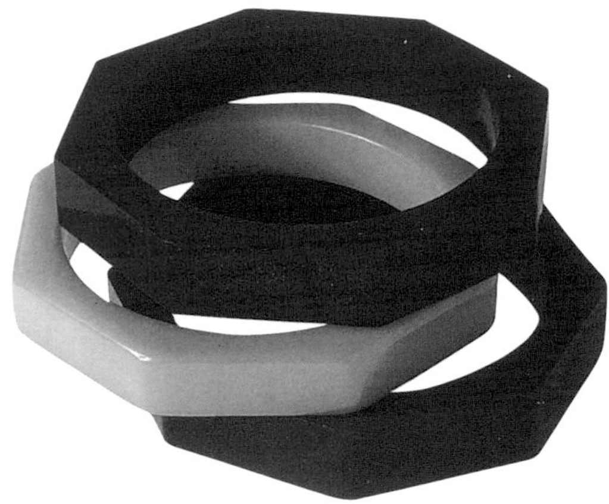

LEFT These hexagonal bracelets in contrasting colours were a fun, inexpensive and popular accessory.

BELOW This brown bangle was carved with organic, flowing leaf-shapes using the tracery method.

BACKGROUND
These stretchy bracelets are made from old Bakelite domino pieces. While the pieces are old, the designs are new, giving rise to the term 'new Bakelite'.

Elastic bracelet

The elastic or 'stretchy' bracelet is exactly what it sounds like – it's a conglomeration of Bakelite pieces that have been drilled and then linked together with elasticized string or thread that has been drawn through the holes and knotted.

Where this idea came from is unknown, but as a functional innovation it allowed large-handed women to wear bracelets, and as stylish innovation it meant that bracelets could be fitted snugly around the wrist or upper arm, if desired.

For the most part, the individual elements of an elastic bracelet are very simple, usually without carving though some have been faceted. A popular style consisted solely of a number of pieces of rod stock cut to length, drilled and strung.

On a more unusual note, you may see bracelets or bangles that have cut into 'slices' or sections and then strung together with elastic string. Such elastic bracelets may be intricately carved.

Should you ever want to create an elastic bracelet, remember this: the area around a drill hole will take over a year to return to the same colour as the outer area of the Bakelite item.

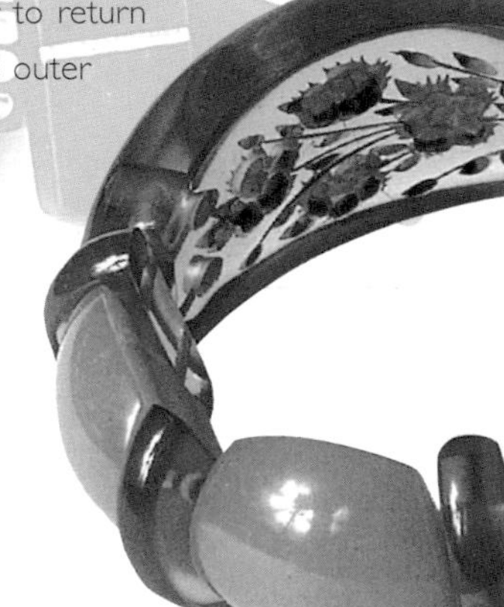

LEFT Bakelite domed-disks mounted on metal findings indicate that this stretchy bracelet originated in Europe.

LEFT Stretchy bracelets are in the main simply designed and consist of plain, geometric shapes.

RIGHT AND FAR RIGHT Cylindrical tubes or a mixture of tubes and half-disks are the basis for these bracelets.

RIGHT As with all things Bakelite, designers could not help but render the simple into the fantastic as this faceted stretchy bracelet displays.

BELOW Carving is rare, but examples do crop up occasionally, like these lovely and highly-sought after reverse-carved, medallion bracelets.

BELOW RIGHT Original Bakelite mah jongg pieces given a recent and second lease of life in stretchy and chain-linked bracelets, pins and pierced earrings.

Stripes

BELOW A streamlined pair of warm two-toned striped bracelets.

The geometric approach of the Art Deco era exhibited itself in the form of stripes, dots and faceting.

The most common method of forming stripes was to laminate three or more pieces of Bakelite tube stock to form a multi-coloured pattern. Most times uncarved, there was the 'can't leave it alone' breed of designers who just had to gild the lily with faceting or scoring the surface in a lathe. There was also the rings of Saturn-style bracelet that resembles pictures of the planet with the many rings which surround it.

ABOVE Striped bracelets in contrasting colours. Note that the two hinged bracelets have some light, criss-cross carving.

Geometrics

The geometric style of the Art Deco era was adapted to Bakelite jewellery in several different ways. Some of the better-known and adventurous designers of this era took on the task of associating their names with that of Bakelite. One of the foremost was a New York designer, Belle Kogan who took the polka dot (see pages 26–27) and stretched it out into an oval, and progressively elongated this figure.

Some of the Belle Kogan bracelets contained a series of 2.5cm (1in) ovals, others may have had 5cm (2in) ovals, right up to the point where two ovals were used to completely encircle a single bracelet.

The bracelets, all in a two-tone motif, were produced by taking a blank from a phenolic tube, carving out the appropriate oval, and mould-injecting a

different colour phenolic into the void. The end-product was then ground flush, the edges were eased, and the piece went to the tumblers for sanding and polishing. These pieces are somewhat rare and are still a very desirable find for collectors today.

During the early 1950's this mould-injection process was carried even further and the result were the gumdrop (multi-coloured and variously-sized dots) bracelets and the much sought after bow-tie bracelets.

The Philadelphia Style

The Philadelphia-style has become a much treasured geometric icon. This style, which conssits of five triangular or disk-shaped pieces bonded together and stuck to the top of a hinged bracelet earned its name and reputation at an antiques show in Philadelphia. A dealer offering a bracelet for sale was amazed when a bidding war erupted. It has since been known as the 'Philadelphia Bracelet'.

MIDDLE Having the same Art Deco design roots as the Belle Kogan bracelets, this pair of geometric bracelets have been carved and cut-through.

LEFT A magnificent collection of oval and elongated oval-patterned Belle Kogan bracelets, beautifully rounded and highly-polished.

RIGHT Smooth and rounded, or flat-sided or shaped, thin or chunky, polka dot bracelets are a visual feast.

Polka dots

Possibly one of the most whimsical designs of the era are the polka dot bracelets. The primary method of manufacture was to drill holes in a somewhat thick blank using an indexing head and a counter-bore. Rods of contrasting colours were then driven into the holes, cut off, ground down, tumbled and then polished.

Generally, these funky pieces were done in boldly contrasting colour schemes – black with white (now turned with time a mustard hue) and black with pink (now orange) were popular.

BELOW A striking statement is made when the polka dots are in strident contrast to their background.

Unfortunately the polka dot has caught the brunt of the scare about the presence of 'new Bakelite' on the market. At some shows, it has become a rarity even to sell one of these

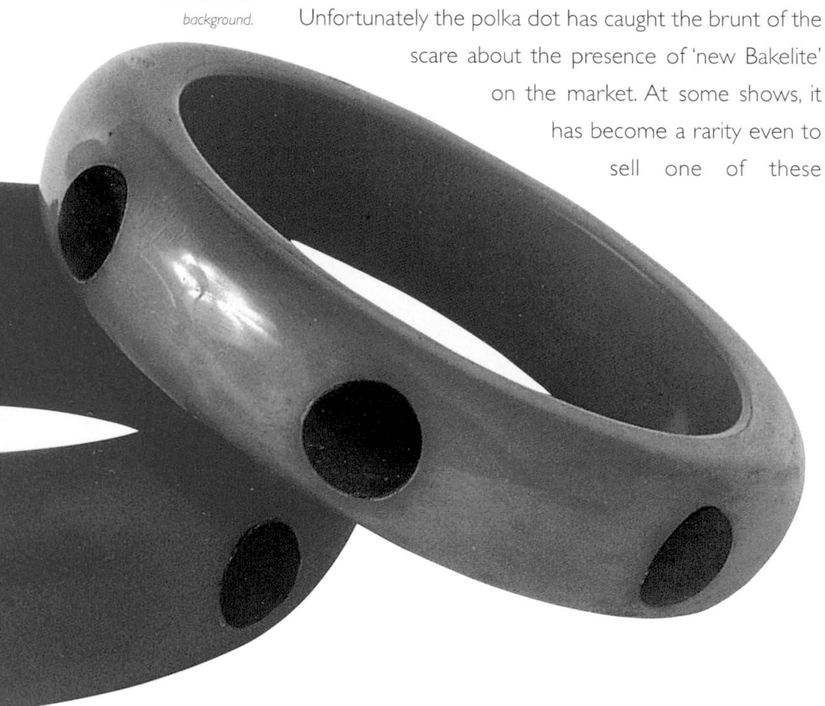

undoubtedly beautiful polka dot bangles because some dealers have scared collectors by telling them the pieces are 'new.' (old bakelite redesigned into a new form).

There was an instance in 1994 when a proud owner of two polka dot bracelets recently purchased for a fair price from a flea market took them to a dealer, only to be told that they were 'new Bakelite.' Her purchases were, in fact, sound but collectors must always be on the watch for unscrupulous dealers, dealing unsound advice or driven by misguided motives.

If as a collector or fashion-conscious consumer, you come across a polka dot piece that you love and can afford, just got for it. The pleasure of owning one or more of these wacky bracelets outweighs purist ideals.

LEFT You could go dotty just looking at these bangles with clear and opaque, and rounded and elongated polka dot inserts.

BELOW Plain, solid colours were often replaced with see-through or marbled-type Bakelite.

Hinged bracelets

These Bakelite wonders seemed to come alive as the dealers found the 'to die for' carvings that collectors were seeking. Originally the appeal of hinged bracelets was limited to the fashion-conscious with large hands over which not even stretchy bracelets would pass. The wearing of a single, elegant hinged bracelet for a formal occasion has overtaken the 'stack them high' brigade who wear bracelets wrist to elbow and make an effort to get them banging together for the 'clunky' noise. The famed 'Philadelphia Bracelet' (see page 23) was, of course, a hinged bracelet with geometric design.

The hinged bracelet is the by-product of cutting a tube in half and ultimately rejoining the two pieces with a spring-loaded hinge. The hinge is usually fastened to the Bakelite with screws or pins. The unhinged ends open so that it slides across the wrist and snaps shut.

Hinged bracelets are designed to fit snugly around the wrist so oval-shaped tubing is preferred. If circular tubing is used, four cuts are made into the tube to create just two usable sections, which when placed end-to-end form an oval.

The two pieces that were used to make up a hinged piece are first carved. Some were carved only on the top section, while others had the bottoms shaped or carved according to the fancy of the worker. After carving, the pieces would be tumbled and polished. The final task was to secure the hinge.

RIGHT A group of four heavily-carved bracelets with relief patterns of flowers, leaves and organic motifs.

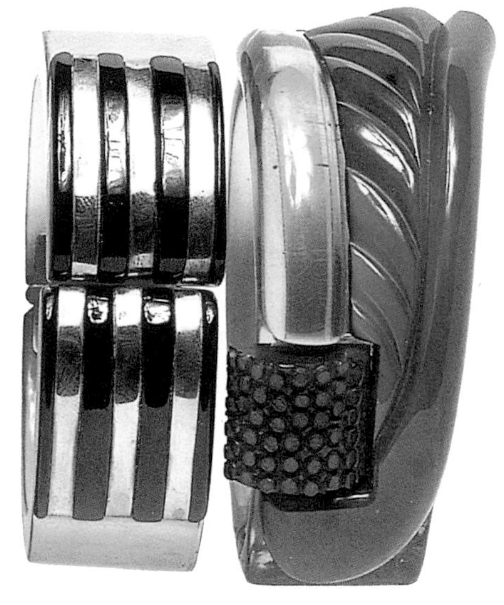

LEFT Hinged bracelet design that knows no limits is shown in these five extraordinary and highly-coveted geometric and laminated bracelets, possibly of European origin.

BELOW From left to right some intricately carved examples of hinged bracelet design from Germany, France and the United States.

LEFT An example of simple but elegant vine work. Note the circular carvings that resemble bunches of grapes.

BOTTOM LEFT The clear, unpigmented secretaries' hinged bracelet is an exquisite example that commands high prices from collectors the world over.

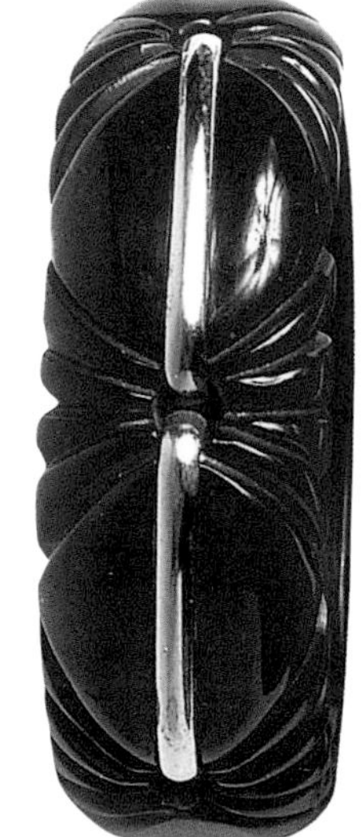

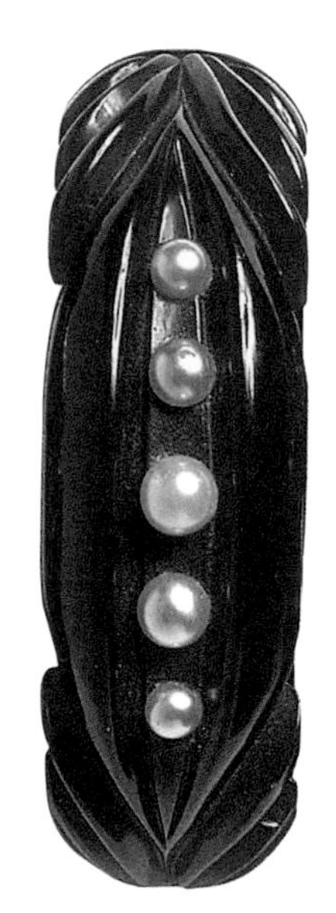

Bangles

Bangles, the simplest form of Bakelite jewellery being just slices off a phenolic tube, hit the fashion scene in the mid-Twenties. The fashionable woman of the post-war 1920s wanted costume jewellery to complement her attire and suit the tightening budgets leading up to the Great Depression. For a time, women had to settle for imitation jet, amber, ivory, and tortoiseshell; the authentic items were simply unaffordable.

During the Roaring Twenties, it was agreed that eight to ten thin, multi-coloured bangles worn around each wrist finished off a costume. Many women also enjoyed the relaxing, clunking sound made by the bangles bumping together.

Novelty companies in America would buy cast tubes of Bakelite in many different colours, slice thousands of bracelets from them, polish the edges and then sell them to the five-and-dime stores or to costume houses such as Coro or Trifari.

The bangles were produced in various thicknesses and edges were either squared or rounded. It is still possible to get hold of bangles that have never been worn and come complete with the original foil label of the costume house, for a reasonable price.

LEFT Faceted clear bangles show the variety of the sizes and colours produced. Cheap and cheerful, as many as eight would be worn on one arm.

RIGHT These bangles show the progression from plain and unadorned to heavily-carved with flower designs.

From the uncarved bangle, jewellery-makers developed pieces that had been turned and carved on a lathe to give the piece a bit of dimension. A couple of scored lines soon became more complicated to create a faceted surface or a single-dimension flower and leaf decoration. This design is plentiful and is most probably inspired by the Art Nouveau era. With cost always the bottom line, such designs could be jigged without extensive time or labour. Colour was as important as ever with translucent and opaque, and single and multi-coloured styles available.

LEFT The ridged effect was achieved by turning the bangles on a lathe. It is possible that these examples were dyed after carving.

LEFT Opaque bangles with various sizes of faceting, some honeycomb-like, others much more pronounced.

As the skills of the carvers grew keener, bangles wore coats of finely- or dramatically-carved scenes. It is not uncommon to find a beautifully-carved panorama, for example, of a seascape with palm trees, setting sun and a wheeling bird. Bangles were also carved to give the spiky texture of a pineapple.

Other bangles designs worth mentioning corresponded to the geometric patterns of Art Deco and to the gears-and-sprockets motifs of the Machine Age.

BELOW Single-colour bangles that were turned on a lathe.

BELOW The ridges created by a lathe have been partially-filled with plastic-coated string. This green bracelet is an excellent example of the form.

RIGHT Impressive towers of white and butterscotch, heavily-carved bangles. The white bangles have darkened due to oxidation.

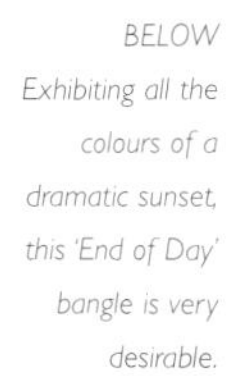

BELOW Exhibiting all the colours of a dramatic sunset, this 'End of Day' bangle is very desirable.

BELOW LEFT Examples of some thick bangles carved with flower and leaf patterns.

BELOW More flower and leaf pattern bangles, but note the cut-through carving, intricacy and almost sculptural look.

Fantasy bracelets

Fantasy bracelets encompass the crazy, wacky, fun pieces that have become so collectable. Bakelite designers certainly cannot be criticized for taking themselves too seriously for their motifs included fruits and vegetables, dominoes and mah jongg pieces, sailing paraphernalia, and heraldic crests mounted on colourful disks. In the main, these mini-Bakelite 'sculptures' were hung from a metal or a celluloid chain to form dangling charm bracelets.

Unfortunately, fantasy pieces are very rare today. By virtue of their design they were extremely fragile, easily broken and less likely to withstand the test of time, so they now command high to exorbitant prices at auction or from dealers.

ABOVE Whatever the design roots of this charm bracelet of contrasting disks, it is striking and stunning in its simplicity.

TOP Charm-type bracelet with oranges and leaves hung from a metal chain.

RIGHT Charm bracelet with an oriental theme. The backings for the metal motifs are Bakelite.

Children's bracelets

At first glance a small-diameter circle of Bakelite may be taken as a napkin ring when it is in fact a child's bracelet. Generally, these pieces are two centimetres or four centimetres in width, and while most are plain some are heavily carved.

BELOW Children's bracelets (also called maiden's bracelets), carved and plain. The black bracelet is adult sized.

RIGHT On the left are the children's bracelets, and on the right is an adult version of the same design.

CHAPTER THREE

RINGS AND EARRINGS

Rings and earrings are the icing on the cake when it comes to Bakelite jewellery – the final adornments to complete an outfit.

There are a few drawbacks for the collector who decides to concentrate on Bakelite rings. The first is finding ones that fit – wearing your collection is just one of the perks of being a jewellery collector. The original rings were usually made to slide onto fingers thinner than today's average. The second drawback is being lucky enough to procure carved rather than the more prevalent plain ones. The final and most daunting drawback is finding rings to start with. Small items, such as rings and earrings tend to go astray while larger items, such as bracelets and necklaces make it back into the jewellery box.

One speciality area is prison rings. The prison ring is in itself an oddity having been fabricated in prisons throughout the United States, although there is one fine example from Europe, possibly the original property of a POW. Prison rings served as a remembrance of the individual whose image is carried on the ring.

Most prison rings have men's photographs embedded in the face (these rings were small and intended for female fingers), but large-diameter rings with the faces of children and women can also be found. The latter ones were most probably made by the inmate for his own wearing.

ABOVE AND LEFT Ring design mirrored other jewellery design in its scope. These rings are examples of asymmetrical design.

LEFT Striped rings were made in the same way as striped bracelets. These rings have an inner core of metal.

ABOVE LEFT Art nouveau-inspired ring with floral carving.

ABOVE Polka dots were everywhere, even on rings!

ABOVE This prison ring consists of up to 25 pieces of Bakelite laminated together. As it depicts a man, the intended wearer was a woman.

Prison pieces were fabricated from Bakelite sourced from all manner of objects. The creative prison inmate would salvage the end of his toothbrush, the bottom of a shaving brush, or a fountain pen. One fortunate collector found a ring that was inscribed 'N.C.S.P. '39'. The initials stand for North Carolina State Penitentiary; the numbers refer to the year 1939. This penitentiary ran recreation periods for inmates and among their pursuits was jewellery-making.

Fixing the photograph to the ring was easily solved. With adhesives less abundant, inmates simply burnt a piece of celluloid and used the resulting flowing liquid to fix photographs or to bond layers of Bakelite for intricate laminated pieces.

Ring designs encompass the full range of styles – geometric, stripes, polka dots, faceted and Art Nouveau floral motifs.

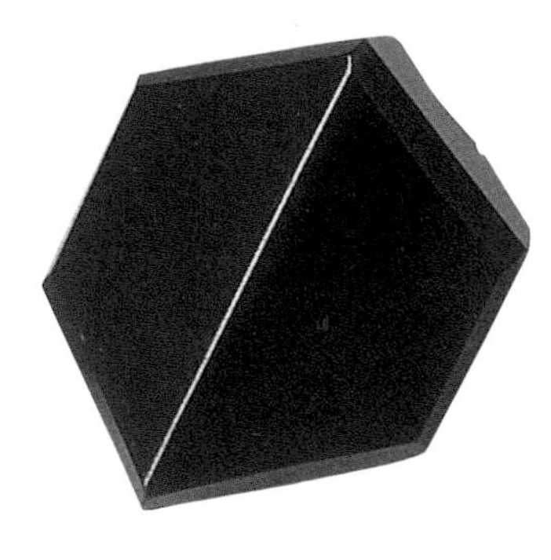

ABOVE This hexagonal ring has been shaped to give two large facets.

BELOW This prison ring with its layers of white celluloid is of particular interest.

ABOVE The image of the inmate would serve to remind a loved one on the outside of the ring's maker.

RIGHT A fun oval shaped ring with a polished marbled effect.

RIGHT A wonderful collection of solid and clear, plain and marbled, smooth and shaped rings in all the colours of the Bakelite rainbow.

Earrings

Bakelite earrings are altogether an easier subject and because they are more plentiful, they are an easily-located item for the collector. They can also be easily worn by the collector.

Earrings come with all kinds of different findings, clips, screw-backs, and the less common, pierced backs. It is also more common to find earrings signed by the designer than, say, a bangle or necklace.

Earring design, like rings, utilized all the styles from the geometric to Art Deco, and you may come across some distinctly theatrical or fantasy pieces – floral bouquets or strands of several beads that hang down to the shoulder. The simplest and most understated were Bakelite beads that had been cut in half and button-like disks that were fixed to clip-on backings or screw-backs.

As a collector, always keep your eyes open for earrings that may complete a parure (a full set of jewellery consisting of matching earrings, necklace, bracelet, ring, belt buckle and brooch).

ABOVE Two modest examples of the string-of-beads type earring. Longer and multi-stranded versions were also made.

BELOW Simulating jade, these earrings have been carved and cut-out to create Oriental-looking faces.

BELOW Two pairs of clear carved earrings. Those on the left bear an Art Deco design, while those on the right are floral.

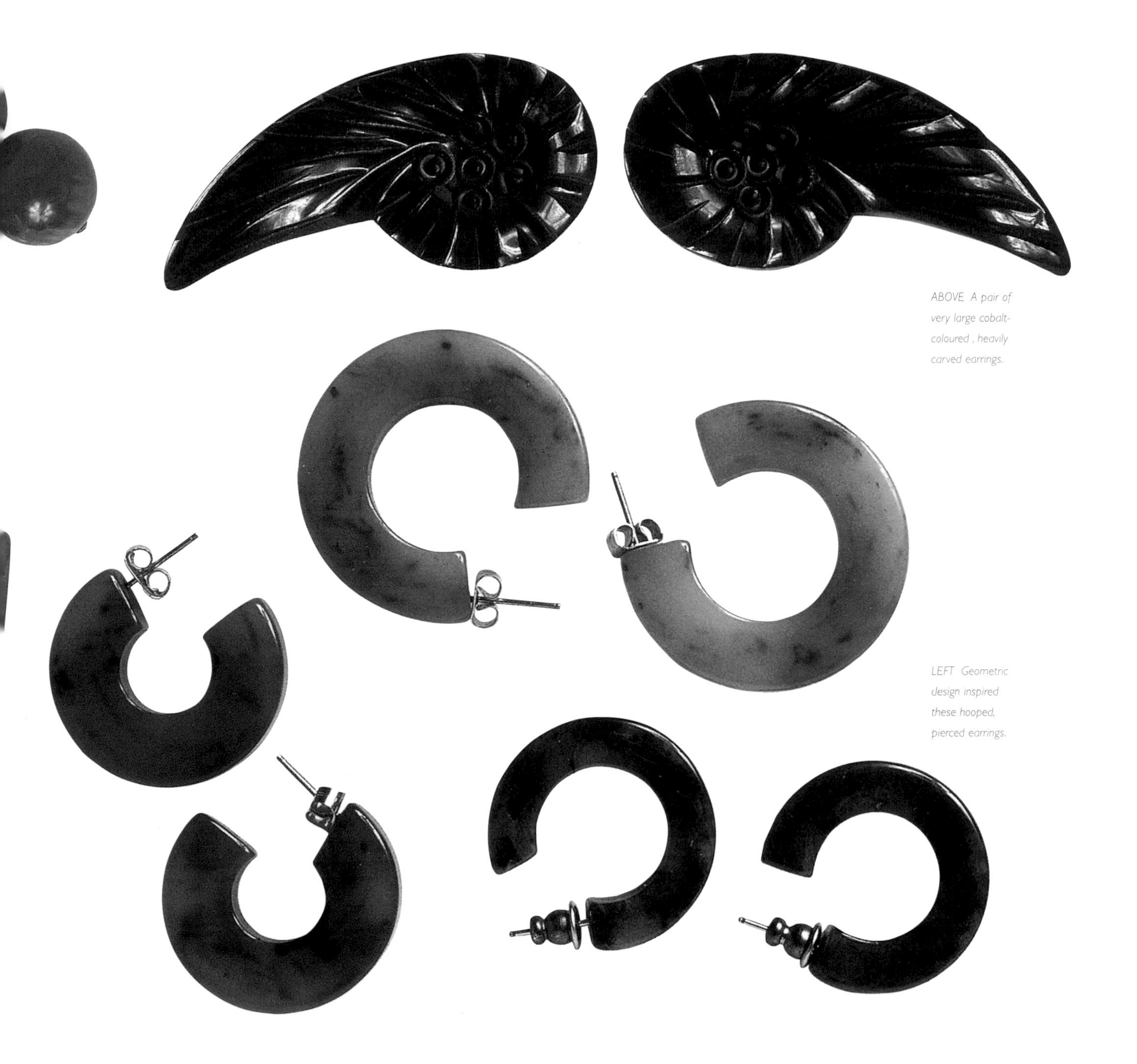

ABOVE A pair of very large cobalt-coloured , heavily carved earrings.

LEFT Geometric design inspired these hooped, pierced earrings.

ABOVE Screw-back earrings with carvings and a strip in a contrasting colour.

ABOVE These clip-on dangling hoops with spherical beads fixed to the findings were all the rage for a period.

LEFT These clip-on dangling earrings were once white.

RIGHT A definite 'must' for the twin-set brigade are these heavily-carved though demure leaf earrings.

C H A P T E R   F O U R

PINS AND BROOCHES

Pins are the devil-may-care members of the Bakelite jewellery family. It was as though they existed purely to fulfil the frustrated dreams and fantasies that bracelet design was unable to grasp.

Mostly composed of cast sheets, the blanks used for carving Bakelite pins vary both in size and thickness. A select few were actually cut from the sides of medium to large tubes. Those wrought from the sides of tube stock display the tell-tale hollow on the underside.

The bar pin was the first of the brooches to be created. At first they were somewhat plain, but later they were carved and eventually took on the shape of ribbons and even bows. The original pins were totally plain white (now mustard), black or brown. As the engineers and chemists advanced the colour range, the pin was givcn a wardrobc of glamourous colours. These were added in layer upon layer during the laminating process.

LEFT The Scottie dog became one of America's most popular designs. It led the pack when it came to animal-inspired jewellery.

ABOVE Imagination ran wild with this pin, possibly of German origin, that has tiny working tools with Bakelite handles. The bar is also Bakelite.

As designers started to bore with the every-day carving of bar pins, they started creating the fantasy pieces we find today. This means that as a collector you can choose a theme, such as cherries or tomatoes, and spend months in search of suitable pieces.

Animal shapes formed a huge proportion of the Bakelite pins which were produced. Some were represented naturalistically, while others were stylized and given personalities. You could wear a favourite creature – a horse, anteater, zebra – or a whimsical family pet or circus creature with great goggly eyes.

In America and Europe during Twenties and Thirties, there was a flurry of animals being produced. Every animal you can think of has been immortalized in a Bakelite pin or brooch. (In the 1980's and early 1990's there was a revival of some of these designs.) Without doubt America's all-time favourite motif – though manufactured in sites around the globe – has been the Scottie dog, fashioned after President Roosevelt's pet Fala. Scottie has been worked in every colour imaginable with detailing ranging from the serious to totally whimsical.

BELOW A pair of matching pins – clear, reversed carved and then painted – that could be fixed to left and right lapels.

ABOVE A large, carved and cut-out floral pin that has been selectively painted.

Pin design rapidly took on lavish carvings as well as some of the motifs of the Machine Age. The designers of pins and brooches seemed to feel particularly unrestricted, allowing their imagination free rein.

When the Machine Age vein branched out from the Art Deco era it took the European market in that direction, while the American craftsmen were left to the 'fun and games' sector of the industry.

Europe enjoyed the angular style, but it was the French who took the design one step further. Their tremendous pieces in vibrant colours had trimmings of Machine Age chrome or twinkling crystal gemstone.

The Germans picked up the idea but substituted chrome with brass. They also took a liking to laminating translucent and opaque colours with clear colours. Some of the most stylistically great pieces attributed to the Germans are the tool pieces, which have a number of tools (that actually work!) with Bakelite handles dangling from a Bakelite bar pin.

BELOW Bar pin showing its European origins by virtue of the brass trimmings.

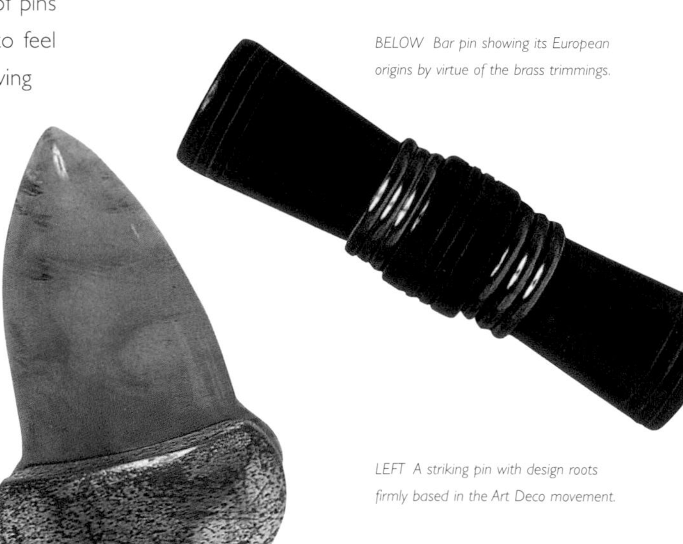

LEFT Fan-style pin of clear Bakelite, carved and painted.

LEFT A striking pin with design roots firmly based in the Art Deco movement.

ABOVE A very simple, tubular bar pin decorated with coils of chrome.

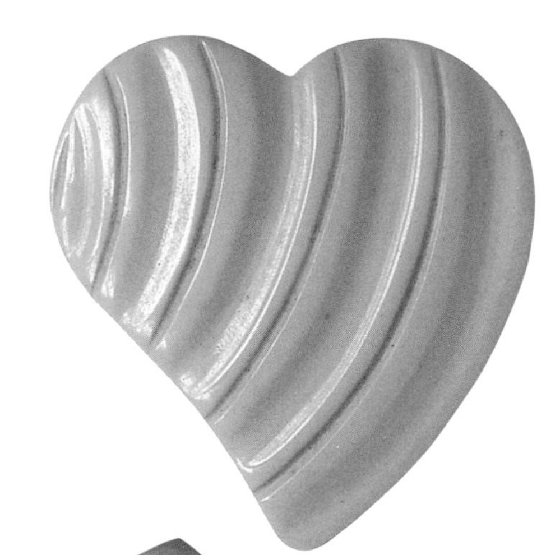

RIGHT This carved, mellow and 'hip' heart pin was once white. Exposure to the elements over time has turned it mustard-coloured.

RIGHT Reversed carved and carved on the front surface, this floral pin has been painted.

LEFT A development of the simple bar pin design, this buckle-like pin has brass trimmings.

ABOVE Classic, angular pin influenced by the Art Deco movement with metal detail down the centre.

RIGHT A heavily-carved bar pin with organic and fern-leaf design.

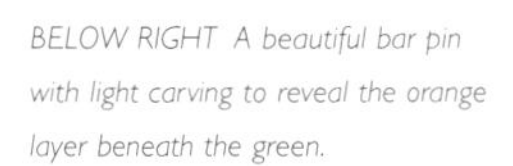

BELOW RIGHT A beautiful bar pin with light carving to reveal the orange layer beneath the green.

LEFT Classic Art Nouveau styling with a prominent chrome centre and brass end-trimmings

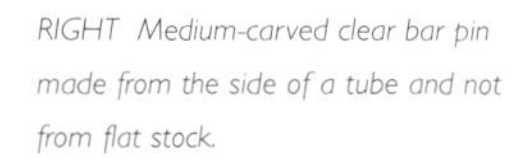

RIGHT Medium-carved clear bar pin made from the side of a tube and not from flat stock.

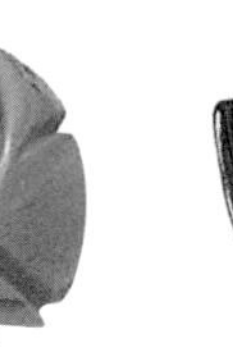

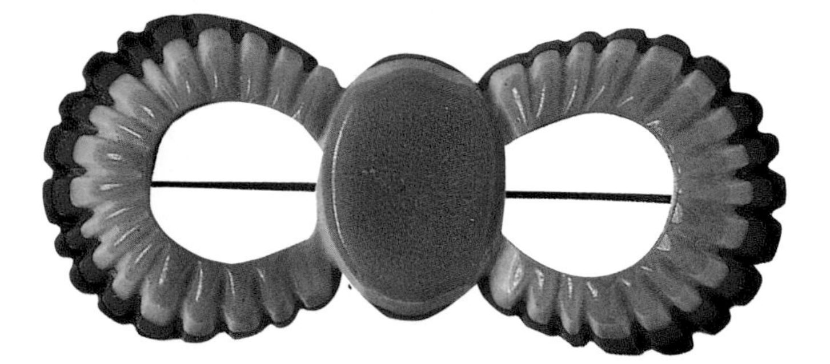

ABOVE RIGHT From the simple bar pin, ornate shapes developed. This one resembles a loosely-tied ribbon bow.

TOP LEFT Another example of the effects of oxidation on white Bakelite.

ABOVE LEFT Laminated layers of different colours are exposed as the bow was carved and shaped.

LEFT An exuberant Art nouveau-inspired design in every respect.

BELOW LEFT A brightly-coloured laminated pin with Art Deco design.

BOTTOM LEFT This oval pin has been studded with brass stars.

BELOW RIGHT Spray design pin resembling a pineapple with its cross-hatched texture and fan of leaves.

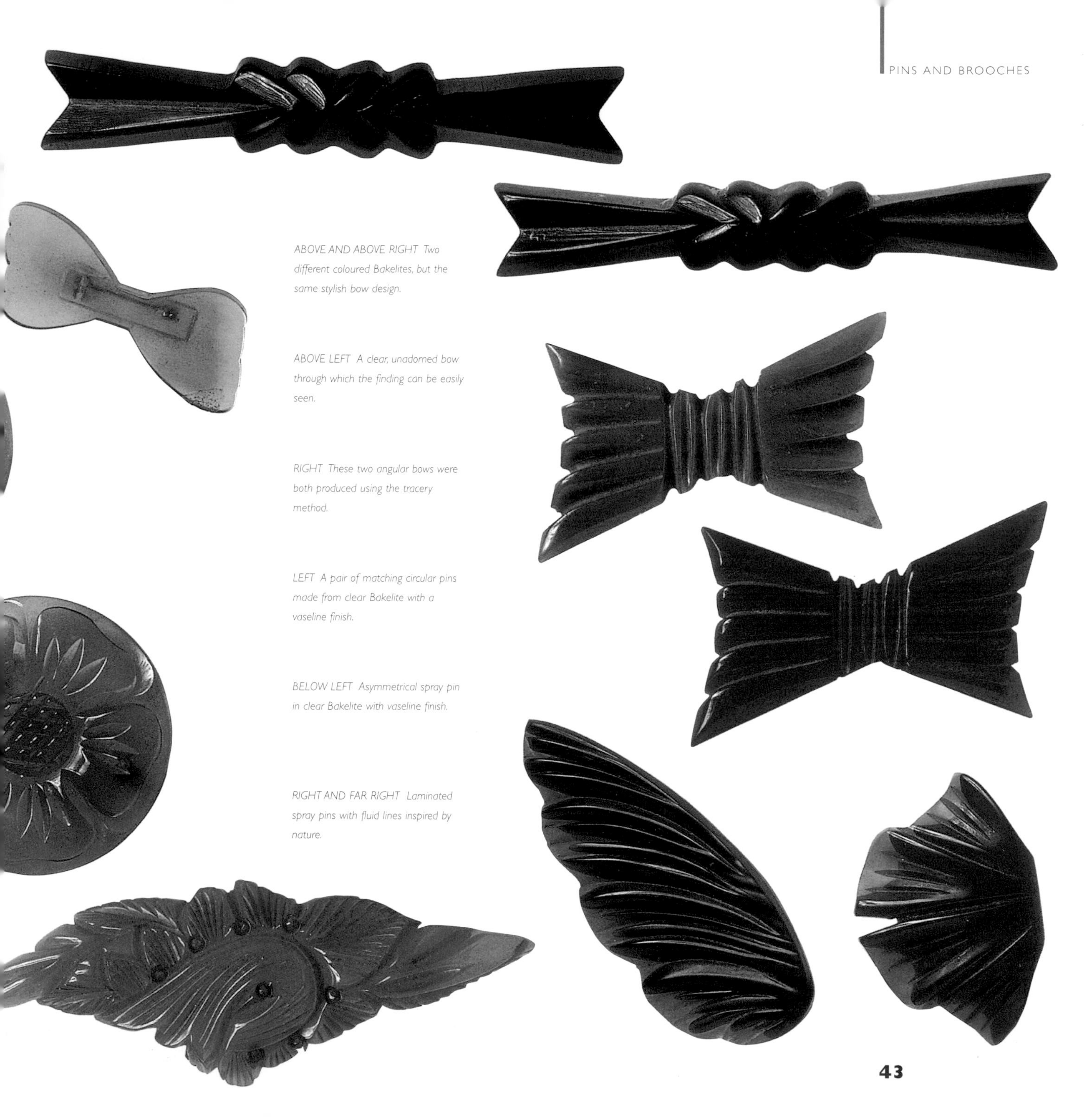

ABOVE AND ABOVE RIGHT Two different coloured Bakelites, but the same stylish bow design.

ABOVE LEFT A clear, unadorned bow through which the finding can be easily seen.

RIGHT These two angular bows were both produced using the tracery method.

LEFT A pair of matching circular pins made from clear Bakelite with a vaseline finish.

BELOW LEFT Asymmetrical spray pin in clear Bakelite with vaseline finish.

RIGHT AND FAR RIGHT Laminated spray pins with fluid lines inspired by nature.

ABOVE LEFT A dangling pin with a heavy geometric design.

ABOVE A stylish pin in the shape of a broadly-brimmed hat. The style is a reminder of the Art Deco era.

FAR LEFT Red and green laminated and shaped base topped with a celluloid cameo. Such designs were influenced by the Victorian revival.

BELOW LEFT Mass production meant that many pins of the same design could be produced. These simple hoops came in a range of colours to match any outfit.

BELOW A realistic, rather than stylized, tri-coloured, hat-shaped pin based on a European theme.

ABOVE A white (now mustard-coloured) and black laminated base with celluloid cameo identical to the one shown left.

BELOW Josephine Baker pin - collector's delight. Born in St Louis, she lived and sang in France, Josephine had pins like this made as gifts. The hat is made of clear Bakelite.

BELOW It is amazing how fruit motifs pervaded every aspect of jewellery design. This classic cherry pin is made of phenolic (leaves and chain) and celluloid(cherries and bar).

ABOVE The subtle patina-tone of the carved Bakelite merges with the brass base on this oval pin.

RIGHT Striking orange base and carved black Bakelite surrounds for the 'Speak no evil, see no evil, hear no evil' monkeys.

BOTTOM RIGHT Tortoiseshell-coloured fish, one of many animal images that were used for pins.

ABOVE RIGHT Inspired by ponies on a carousel, the mane is decorated with brass studs.

TOP Clear, floral pin that has been reverse-carved and the flower painted.

ABOVE LEFT Laminated layers create this hat-shaped pin that has been finished off with fabric flowers.

LEFT Butterscotch-coloured pin with obvious floral carving. The leaves and centre have been painted.

RIGHT This majestic stallion pin which is studded with crystal has matching earrings.

BELOW A vibrant and unmissable floral pin, heavily-carved, with amber-coloured crystal in the centre.

BELOW LEFT Halved beads have many uses; this time it is as a simple, geometric pin.

ABOVE This, believe it or not, is a zebra pin. Just another of the animals immortalized in Bakelite jewellery.

ABOVE RIGHT Resin- washed horse's head with brass tack.

BELOW The ubiquitous Scottie dog rendered in a very angular style and mounted on a chrome base.

BELOW RIGHT A French assembly kit of a Shetland pony with crystals highlighting the eyes, ears, nose, saddle and tail. Sections have been overpainted.

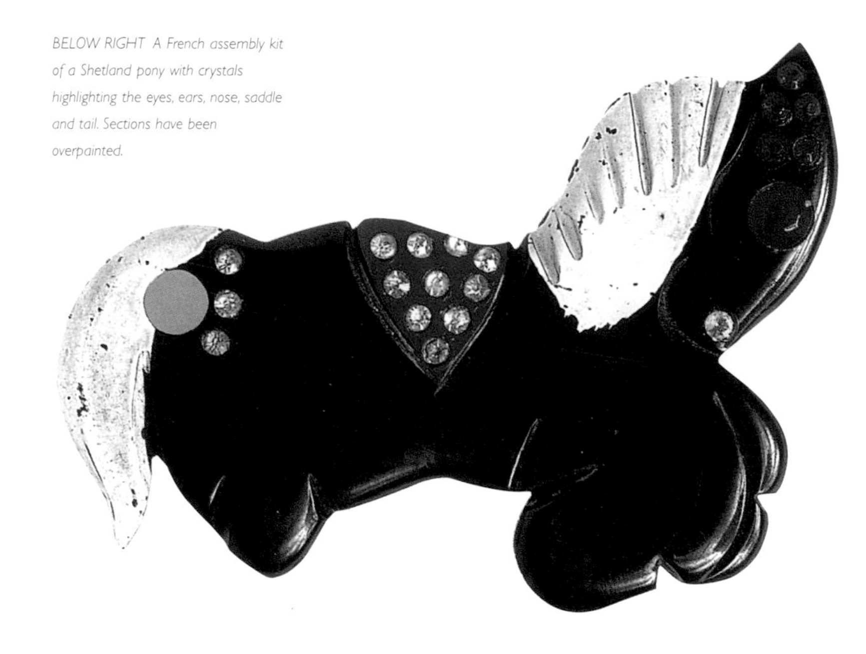

RIGHT A duck pin where the body is of Bakelite but the wing is acrylic.

RIGHT A European design, this gentleman turtle has a deep-red translucent body mounted on brass. A nice touch is the brass chain to the monocle.

LEFT Top cat with wacky goggle eyes, Bakelite head and acrylic body.

ABOVE Clear Bakelite has been used for the body of this exotic bird of European origin. The base, which includes the head, claw, wings and tail, is chrome.

RIGHT The creepy and the fantastical together in these European pins made of Bakelite and brass.

CHAPTER FIVE

BAKELITE ACCESSORIES GALORE

Further evidence of the versatility of Bakelite and how it revolutionized the fashion industry is by how many accessories were made of Baekeland's invention. The range of possibilities includes: belts and belt buckles, dress clips, hat pins, umbrella handles, cuff links, necklace clips, and handbag handles and clasps.

Because of the nature of these pieces, they attracted the attention of carvers and many pieces could be classed as fantasy items.

Belt buckles and dress clips have a tendency to co-ordinate with other pieces of jewellery, and therefore their design imitates those of bangles, pins or brooches.

Every collector's dream is to have a completely matching 10-piece parure consisting of earrings, necklace, pin, dress clips, bracelet, ring, buckle and hair clip. They do exist, but getting all the components in one place is little short of a miracle.

ABOVE This clown design can be found on a belt buckle and a pin. The belt-buckle version is mounted on a rectangle of black.

LEFT Heavily-carved buckles, the first based on a pea-pod with pearls for the peas, that open by unfastening a hook and loop.

TOP AND ABOVE These Bakelite cuff links and necktie pin were mistakenly thought to be made of amber.

TOP RIGHT Three hat pins or shirt decorations were originally white, the Bakelite has since discoloured.

RIGHT Bakelite hinged bracelet with inset watch that apparently still works!

ABOVE A pair of magnificent geometric dress clips, strikingly designed in bold colours and in mint condition.

RIGHT The term 'end of the day', which describes the Bakelite used in the umbrella, refers to the fact that it displays all the colours of a sunset.

LEFT Glamorous beaded handbag with clear Bakelite frame and clasp.

ABOVE Coco Chanel-type dress clips with crystals mounted on Bakelite backings. Examples like this make many look forward to the day when dress clips are once again a fashion necessity.

LEFT An assortment of belt buckles showing different degrees of carving. This distinctive mustard-colour is a sure sign that these were once white.

RIGHT Bakelite rings and disks in red and orange joined by metal links make up this fantastic belt.

CHAPTER SIX

SECRETS OF BAKELITE JEWELLERY COLLECTING

The soundest bit of advice about telling the real McCoy from the impostor is to rub the piece and then smell it. Bakelite has a musty – sometimes described as soapy or resinous – smell due to the phenol content. But a timid rub is not sufficient, give it a hard, fast rub that almost produces blisters on your thumb. When your thumb is hot, smell it and the piece but do it quickly because the odour will dissipate in about two seconds. But beyond smell, use also your senses of sight, touch and hearing to tell the real Bakelite from the fakes.

Novel though the following experiments may be, there is nothing like seeing to make you believe. What you need to do is to buy several inexpensive bangles or other pieces. Explain to the dealer you want to do some experimenting at home. Vary your selection according to the types of plastic, and label each piece according to whether it is Bakelite, celluloid or an acrylic (lucite).

Set up an area for your experiments, making sure surfaces are protected and that a source of running water is nearby. You will need the following: a very stiff toothbrush, flat-jaw pliers (not serrated or tongs), a small sharp knife, a fine-toothed hacksaw blade and sandpapers graded 200, 400 and 600. As you get further into your collecting, add to your stock of tools.

Many believe that the best way to tell Bakelite is to stick a hot pin in it. Forget this – it's dangerous! Should the item be an old piece of celluloid, chances are a fragment

BELOW When you start your collection you may be attracted by certain designs or colours, or your collection could be based on function.

RIGHT Carved bracelet with acorn and oak leaf 'charms'. The links are made of celluloid.

of celluloid will fly and out, it will ruin an otherwise lovely piece. Also older celluloid is cellulose nitrate – nitrate is an explosive. If the piece is made of Bakelite, sticking a hot pin in to it will do nothing except leave a tiny burgundy or purple dot. (Burgundy or purple being the colours of burnt Bakelite). So put away the needle, and try these sound and safe ways of checking the veracity of a piece.

Sense of smell

Place the Bakelite piece under scalding-hot, running water for about 30 seconds and then quickly smell it. The hot water should release the phenol smell. If not, then dip it in to boiling water and smell it again. If the piece is Bakelite or another phenolic, this will surely release the odour.

Once you get the smell of phenol, you will never forget it. This can be your rule of thumb when you are buying pieces for your collection: if it has the familiar phenol odour when you rub it with your thumb (see page 53) you cannot go far wrong.

The next step is to take the pieces that you have labelled celluloid and acrylic, and dip these in extremely hot water. The celluloid will emit a slight camphor smell, while a smell somewhat similar to automobile oil will rise from the acrylic.

ABOVE A once white hinged bracelet and pin set with black Bakelite ovals and celluloid cameos.

Feel to believe

You can also train yourself to recognize the feel of genuine Bakelite. Once the items that you are using for your experiments have cooled, vigorously rub each piece with a thumb. Doing this after the pieces has been dipped in hot water will mean that layers of wax and polish will have been removed to reveal the material's true texture. Waxed Bakelite is smooth and slippery, while stripped Bakelite has an abrasive feel.

While rubbing the piece, you should notice that your thumb will heat up rather quickly with the Bakelite, and that other plastics will feel more slippery to the touch.

ABOVE The front and back (showing the original finding) of a button. The decoration is a stylized flower with long stamens.

Again, as you rub you will smell phenolic resin in the Bakelite, whereas you will never attain a smell from cooled thermoplastics.

Next, take all the pieces and drop them into a container of hot water for about three to five minutes. Retrieve them with pliers, and as soon as they are cool (but not cold) enough to handle try to bend, twist and knead them. You will notice that the thermoplastics have become pliable and the thermoset phenolics are rigid.

Sounds like Bakelite

Hold a Bakelite piece lightly between a thumb and forefinger. Gently tap the piece against another piece of Bakelite. The resulting sound – a dull, hollow, thud sound – is similar to the tapping of two pieces of bamboo. With time and practice you'll be able produce this distinctive sound simply by flicking the piece with a fingernail. When you repeat the procedure with the celluloid and plastics you should notice that the sound they make is more of a higher-pitched, 'clacking'.

LEFT A four-piece set in translucent burgundy and brass trim. This set most probably heralded from Germany.

Under close inspection

RIGHT This pin is not Bakelite but moulded celluloid. The giveaway is a mould hole that can be seen below the pin fastening.

When you have a piece of jewellery that you know for certain is Bakelite, but the sound is not quite right look closely to see if it has been cracked or carries a repair. Cast bangles have a tempered-like quality and when cracked or repaired they never regain that bamboo sound. This up-close inspection will also prevent you unwittingly buying damaged or badly repaired pieces.

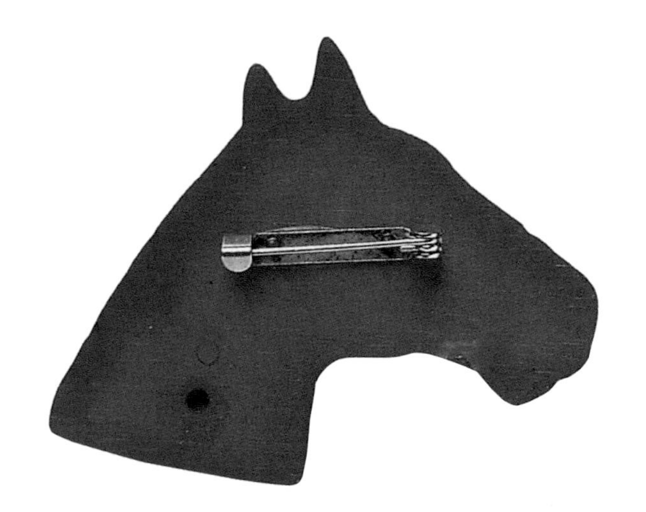

BELOW A selection of clear reverse-carved and painted bracelets. Like many reverse-carved pieces, the decoration is floral.

Starting your collection

If such an enthralling and engrossing subject as Bakelite jewellery can be reduced to three points, these are the ones to bear in mind when collecting:

1 Find a dealer who has a large inventory of at least 100 pieces of Bakelite. If they have other plastics this is an extra feather in their cap as it most probably indicates a wide-ranging knowledge and interest. A good dealer will take the time to help you, not just try to sell you something.

2 Don't be embarrassed or talked into buying a piece. If you are not sure, then go with your intuition.

3 Select an area of Bakelite jewellery to concentrate on. You can collect pieces of a certain colour, a certain design, or make an eclectic collection of bangles, rings or whatever. Give yourself a budget and make sure that you stick to it. As well as preventing you overspending it may also help to determine the type of pieces that you collect.

The mental process, probably the most interesting part of collecting, is as varied as the collectors themselves. Some collections start with multi-coloured laminated pins and hinged bracelets and then move in the direction of clear but 'carved to death' pieces. Then without rhyme or reason, one pattern of carving strikes a chord and then the collection is culled to leave a pure collection of that particular design.
So do not be surprised if your collection changes – the hunt is often the most exciting aspect.

Collectors mostly indulge in a whimsical manner. Some collect figurals, others a particular style or colour; many are keen on pieces in the shape of fruit and vegetables. There are also the parure collectors who are constantly on the prowl for that pin that will perfectly match the necklace, bracelet, earrings and dress clips.

ABOVE A first glance this looks like an eclectic collection of bracelets and bangles, but all the pieces are in fact European, mostly from France.

BELOW Belt buckle with stylized floral pattern. Always check the findings and fastenings to see if they are original.

The beauty of collecting Bakelite is that there are no boundaries, and once you have put together one collection you can shift into another assortment.

Is it old or new?

This question is not a simple one. It is similar to asking is a piece made of old or new amber? Amber, in order to evolve into its present form, has let nature take the sap from a tree, and compress and petrify it for thousands of years. Just how do you classify anything so old as new? Although cuttings and the sweepings of amber are ground and emulsified and sold as reprocessed amber, it is still amber.

Bakelite is similar. All of the Bakelite jewellery that you see today is old Bakelite. It was cast from the mid-Twenties up until the early Forties when the formula was sold to Union Carbide. (A purchase possibly made in order to facilitate the marketing of cheaper plastics manufactured by Union Carbide at the time.) The Marblette company produced it until the early Fifties. There is no company producing cast phenolic jewellery today. This is because of the cost of processing and the raw materials. In addition, the machines, jigs and vacuum systems (the fine dust produced when carving must not be ingested) used in the carving process, as well as the polishing tumblers have mostly gone to the scrapyard.

Rumours about a new Bakelite being in circulation abound. There are a few dealers who claim every piece you show them is 'new Bakelite' and they would, of course, take it off your hands for a pittance. If you were so unwise you could return to their shop the next day and see your piece carrying a much-inflated price tag.

Colour changes

The long and the short of it is that the bulk of what is called 'new Bakelite' is in fact another polymer. The difference can be detected in many ways.

The presence of the colour white is an immediate indicator. There is no longer a white-coloured Bakelite. Over time and with constant exposure to the elements white Bakelite turns a mustard colour. It can be returned to its original colour

BELOW Pin, bracelet and earrings in matching translucent burgundy and bearing the same carving.

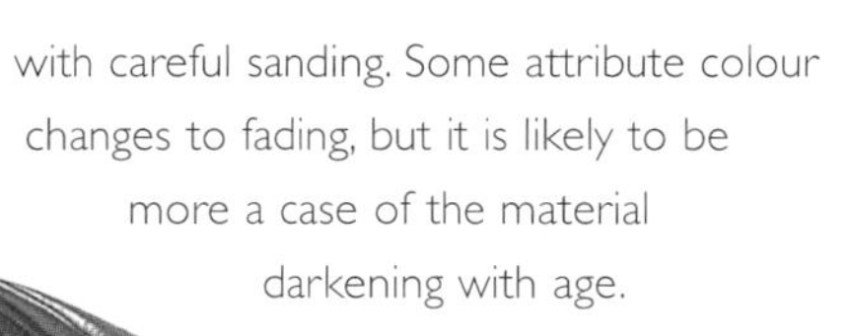

LEFT Matching pin and belt buckle – the first two pieces in what could be a ten-piece set.

with careful sanding. Some attribute colour changes to fading, but it is likely to be more a case of the material darkening with age.

Take a piece of Bakelite jewellery and find an inconspicuous area and sand it with grade 200 paper. You will be amazed to find that the mustard colour will turn to white; weird, dark green colours will lighten to a rich cobalt; lighter oranges will shine a pastel pink; greens turn a light jade colour; and light greenish-orange will become a light blue. If you finish the sanded area with very fine grade sandpaper and leave it on your windowsill, in 30 days you will be hard pressed to figure out where you sanded because it will have reverted to its original colour.

Bangles, rings and napkin rings demonstrate this colour change process. If you look inside the piece, then outside you will find the inner areas much lighter than the exposed outer area. You may come across bangles that have assumed an odd colour, don't be put off the piece immediately. Chances are that the colour change has occurred because of contact with perfume or another chemical.

Something old is new again

Over time you will find quite a few examples of what could be referred to as newly-manufactured items from old pieces of Bakelite. There are people who comb the old findings in warehouses throughout the country in search of old Bakelite parts. These 'new' pieces are generally found at flea markets with pendants being especially common. Often original Bakelite buttons are made into earrings.

The best way to tell whether you are looking at a piece of 'recycled' Bakelite is to look at the findings or fastenings used. New findings (which were purchased at the local craft shop) will be hot-glued or superglued onto an old piece of Bakelite. As neither of these adhesives existed at the time when the Bakelite was produced, you can be sure that it is a 'new' piece.

An original construction would consist of a pin-back of two separate components, set into holes drilled into the Bakelite. Another method used is two tabs on the back of the pin-back, which were pressed into holes drilled at back angles; the tabs would have then been pressed back into the angle of the holes. The third method was a bar pin that has rivets or screws,

BELOW Identical bangles in every way except colour. Once you get this far on a special collection, it is hard to give up on it.

fastening the pin to the body. Giveaways for necklaces are the chains that were used. The greatest amount of neckware produced in the Twenties and Thirties used celluloid chains, with some American and many German designers preferring to use solid brass chains. Some French designers used chromium-plated brass and copper for chains as well as accent parts. If pin-backs or chains do not fall into one of these categories, then you should take a much closer look. You will also see jewellery that was made from gaming pieces – for example, mah-jongg and domino bracelets, with pins and earrings to match. The bulk of the dealers know what is original, and can tell you the story behind each piece.

RIGHT AND BELOW Tortoiseshell-coloured paddles suspended from celluloid link chains make up this necklace and matching pin.

Ron and Esther Shultz

This husband-and wife team from Pennsylvania dedicated themselves to reworking and making Bakelite jewellery from salvaged pieces of Bakelite.

LEFT This beautiful brooch with the distinctive Bakelite colours is polished to a high lustre which is typical of the Shultz pieces.

The Shultzs buy any old pieces of Bakelite they can find. It may be a cracked radio cabinet or a broken piece of jewellery, but Ron or Esther can transform this discarded item into a piece of art. They not only copy some of the well-known pieces, but have also used their imaginations to create their own unique designs.

They are both justifiably very closed-mouthed as to the methods they use, but to the untrained eye it is hard to tell which pieces have been recently created. To their credit, their booth at shows is covered with signs explaining that their work is 'new work from old pieces', and that copies are made to a slightly different scale so that they will not be confused with the originals.

RIGHT A clear bangle with a fish motif and black edging crafted from recycled Bakelite.

For many years their work was minus their signature, but that changed in around 1993 when a signed label was adhered to pieces. The couple now engrave their names deep into each piece. Even though each piece is a labour of love, their prices are very reasonable. So reasonable that a sort of cult is taking form, with people building collections that consist of strictly Shultz originals or copies.

Shultz pieces are easily spotted – just look for the exaggerated lustre of the finish. This could possibly be due to meticulous sanding with 1600 grade sandpaper followed by polishing with a jeweller's rouge to accomplish the glass-like texture. Bakelite was tumble-polished in the Thirties but this method could never achieve the over-polishing found on a Shultz creation.

Where to look

The best place to start your Bakelite collection would probably be at an antiques show. The main reason for this is that while you are still a novice, you want to deal with people who know what they have and can prove to you that what they are selling is what they are representing it to be.

BELOW A clear Bakelite watch pin with leaf design drop suspended on squared metal links.

Dealers who attend antiques shows are usually in the business for the long haul, and therefore you will be able to get in touch with them again at a later date should you have any problems or queries. They are also constantly trying to generate new business. For example, when you decide to graduate into bigger and better pieces, they will often take some of your earlier, less elaborate or more common pieces in trade for that piece you have been covetting for some time. Your old, less valuable pieces will provide the dealer with suitable stock for newer collectors.

You will pay a little more at antiques shows because the dealer incurs higher overheads, but you will benefit in the long run. You can make a dependable friend who will help you through the infancy of your collection. A good dealer will keep in contact with you and call when he or she picks up that piece that you so desperately seek.

Experienced shopper

After you have been collecting for a while and you feel more confident, then it is time you foraged through the flea markets, church sales and junk shops, rubbing elbows with those obsessed with finding the ultimate treasure for short money. In these places, you will generally find mediocre pieces at reasonable prices. What every collector dreams of is stumbling across the great Bakelite piece that has been labelled lucite, celluloid or even wood in error. If it happens, it is a day you will never forget.

Outside dealers

Dealers in other fields will often knowingly come across Bakelite in a house lot they have purchased, but they will sell it very cheaply because they did not pay as much as a Bakelite dealer would have to. When dealing primarily in Bakelite, the dealer pays more in order to keep a large and varied inventory.

Keep an eye out for any Bakelite that is being sold cheaply, You can often use them to sell to a more novice collector, or you can use them for barter.

RIGHT Two identical white (now yellow) bracelets with oriental theme and inlaid stones.

Keeping track

Try to keep track of the price trends in your area of collecting through attending collectors shows and talking to dealers. This way you can establish a guide for yourself when you set out to buy a special piece or want to sell an item. If you do not know immediately the price of something and have to go away and check or confer with someone, the piece you want may be gone when you return.

LEFT Pendant and earring prison set made from black Bakelite bonded with white celluloid and topped with mercury cameo.

How much to pay

Because of the large number of variables, the best answer to this question is to pay what you are comfortable with. This means having a budget and then sticking to it.

There are times, though, when budget considerations just go out of the window. If a piece you find is rare, in pristine condition, in a highly-desirable colour, it is likely that you will spend top dollar. If it is in poor condition or, more importantly, damaged, then the price should be drastically reduced. Items can be repaired to give you a great Bakelite addition to your collection at an extremely reduced cost. It is fine if this works out, but beware of investing heavily in a piece that will not recover your outlay.

'New' or custom-made Bakelite should always be purchased at a reduction in comparison to original pieces. If you find that a dealer is trying to get top price, then he or she is in the business solely for the money.

LEFT Clear, coloured bangles, like this assortment in prime condition, can command premium prices.

How to care for Bakelite

Once overcome with Bakelite fever you will need things to do when the shows pull out of town and the shops are closed. Most collectors take enormous joy and also find it terribly relaxing to polish their collection.

Whenever you find a new piece, whip out a stiff toothbrush and give that piece a hot soapy bath and scrub. Clean off all the dirt and layers of wax and grease, then towel it dry. Apply a healthy amount of polish and get rubbing. Simi-Chrome and Top Bright are commonly used polishes. Both come from Germany and smell, feel and work the same. Canny people have been known to go to auto-body supply shops and buy large tins of quality rubbing or polishing compound for the same price as a small tube of specialist potion.

Rubbing compound worked with a buffing wheel will take out small scratches. If you polish by hand, work the toothbrush and mixture of your choice vigorously into every nook and cranny. Remove any excess polish by scrubbing under very cold water. The last but most satisfying step is buffing the piece to a uniform, rich lustre with an old, soft towel.

Always store Bakelite pieces away from direct sunlight, and when transporting them wrap each piece separately in soft paper or cloth. Even the slightest rubbing of one piece against another will result in dull abrasion marks or chips which reduce its value.

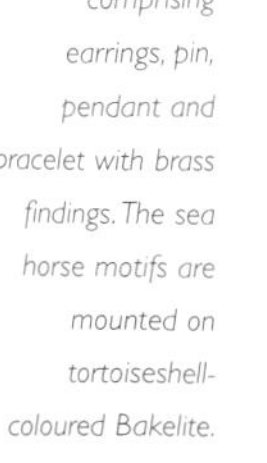

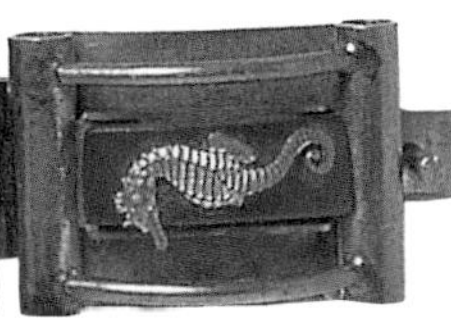

Four-piece set comprising earrings, pin, pendant and bracelet with brass findings. The sea horse motifs are mounted on tortoiseshell-coloured Bakelite.